Funky Junk

♻ Recycle rubbish into art

Funky Junk creations by Gary Kings
Additional text by Richard Ginger
Illustrations by Barry Green

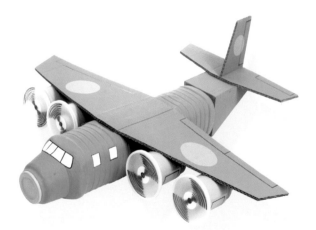

Copyright © 2008 by Top That! Publishing plc
All rights reserved.
This Dover edition, first published in 2012, is a slightly-altered republication of the edition originally published by Top That! Publishing plc, in 2008.
ISBN-13: 978-0-486-49022-9
ISBN-10: 0-486-49022-X
Dover Publications, Inc., Mineola, New York
49022X01

CONTENTS

BEFORE YOU BEGIN

Rubbish, junk, trash—whatever you call it, households throw out hundreds of boxes, bottles, cardboard and cartons every day, which you can transform into an endless array of brilliant models and toys!

This book will show you how.

Before you begin construction you will need to gather together a variety of materials that are heading for the trash can! Once you have a good collection of cartons and containers, you are well on the way to hours of fun making your own recycled creations.

By following the step-by-step instructions in this book, you will soon be transforming old egg boxes into a chunky caterpillar, or this morning's cereal box into a swooping stunt plane. The glossary on page 64 explains many of the terms used in the book—look at this first.

The fantastic thing about all the models is that they will cost you next to nothing! Just make sure you've got glue, paint, paintbrushes, scissors and tape.

So keep your eyes peeled, and next time you see Mom or Dad about to throw out an old yogurt cup shout "Stop!" The more plastic lids, bottles, cartons, buttons, string and containers you can get your hands on, the more your collection of models will continue to grow.

You'll soon discover that a load of old trash can mean hours of fun!

RECYCLED ROBOT

This colorful, recycled robot has an impressive array of gadgets and gizmos that will make him look great on your bedroom shelf. He has a pair of claw hands and jagged jaws that are pretty scary, and he sits on top of some great tank tracks, all ready to roll into battle!

You Will Need:

One cardboard tube (approx 12 in. long)

One large short yogurt cup

Strong white glue

Paint and paintbrushes

Thick plain card

Scissors

Thick cardboard

A black marker pen

Four small plastic lids

Colored card

White paper

Two colored bendy straws

One cardboard box (approx 7 in. x 5 in. x 3 in.)

Yellow paper

Four red bendy straws

Four plastic lids

One cardboard box (approx 10 in. x 5 in. x 3 in.)

One oval plastic container

Six plastic lids

Corrugated card

Red card

Stickers

One small cardboard tube

Two small, thin tubes

Two fabric softener bottle lids

One small soda bottle

MAKING THE HEAD

1 Find a large cardboard tube, approx 12 in. long, and a large yogurt cup. Glue the yogurt cup onto the end of the cardboard tube, as shown, and then paint both of them purple.

2 Scale up and copy the jaw templates (see pages 10–11) onto a sheet of thick card. Ask an adult to help you cut them out. Then, bend the jaw into shape and glue it together, as shown. Now scale up and copy the jaw spacer template onto thick cardboard four times. Cut these out, glue them together and then glue them to the inside of the jaw, as shown.

3 Glue the jaw onto the cardboard tube from step 1. Paint the jaw a light gray color. When this is dry, add details with a black marker pen. Add two small plastic lids to either side of the jaw, as shown.

4 Make two ears for your robot from some colored card. Glue these on either side of the yogurt cup. Cut out and add a couple of eyes made from white paper, and use a black marker pen to add details. Cut down and glue two straws together, as shown. Glue these to the top of your robot's head.

MAKING THE BODY

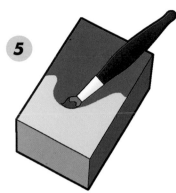

5

5 Find a cardboard box that is approx 7 in. x 5 in. x 3 in. Carefully undo its glued edges and then turn it inside out and glue it all together again. (This gives you a plain surface to paint on.) Now paint it purple.

6 Cut out a rectangle of yellow paper approx 6 in. x 4 in. and round off its corners. Glue it onto the front of the box and then add the details to it with a black marker, as shown.

6

7 Push four red, bendy straws inside one another to form a frame the same size as the yellow rectangle you cut out in step 6. Glue these straws over the rectangle and also add a couple of plastic lids to it, as shown.

7

8 Scale up and copy the ring template provided onto a sheet of thick card twice. Ask an adult to help you cut these out, then glue one to either side of the body, and paint them orange, as shown.

9 Place the long cardboard tube with the head attached to it on the top of the body. Draw around the cardboard tube and then remove it. Cut out the circle on the top of the body and then push the tube as far as you can into the hole, as shown.

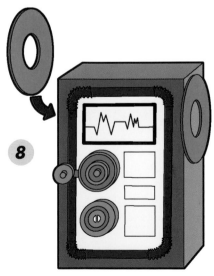

8

9

WHeeLS anD Base

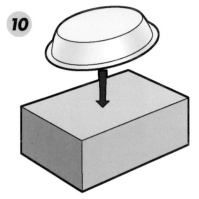

10 Find a cardboard box that is approx 10 in. x 5 in. x 3 in. Carefully undo its glued edges and then turn it inside out and glue it all together again. (This will give you a plain surface to paint on.) Now glue an oval plastic container onto this box, as shown.

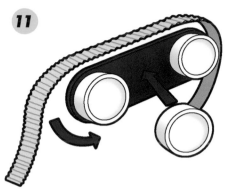

11 Scale up and copy the tank track template provided onto thick card twice. Ask an adult to help you cut them out. Glue three identical plastic lids onto each of these tank tracks. Now cut two long strips of corrugated card 1 in. wide, and wrap one around each tank track, as shown.

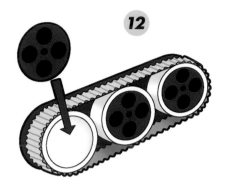

12 Cut out six disks of red card that are slightly smaller than the plastic lids. Detail each of these with a black marker pen, as shown, and then glue them to the plastic lids.

13 Glue the completed tank tracks onto either side of the box from step 10, and then paint everything in bright colors, as shown.

14 Detail the base section of your robot with stickers, colored paper, a marker pen and small plastic lids, as desired.

PUTTING IT TOGETHER

15 Scale up and copy the arm template provided onto a sheet of thick card twice. Cut them out. Cut the small cardboard tube in half. Now cut each half down its length to make two claws. Glue one of these onto each arm. Paint the claws red and the arms orange.

17 Cover two small, thin tubes with red paper. Cut a hole in either side of the body (using the inner circle of the ring parts you stuck on in step 8 as a guide). Push each of the tubes into these holes as far as they will go, as shown. Use glue to stick each arm onto the tubes you have fixed in place. Now glue the completed top section of your robot to the base section you completed in step 14.

16 Fix a fabric softener bottle lid onto each arm by cutting holes in the shoulder areas. Also glue plastic lids to the elbow areas of each arm. Detail each arm with colored paper and a marker pen as desired.

18 Find a small brightly colored drink bottle or paint a plain one in a color of your choice. Decorate the bottle with bits of colored card and add details with a black marker pen. Use white glue to fix the bottle on the back of your robot, to create a backpack.

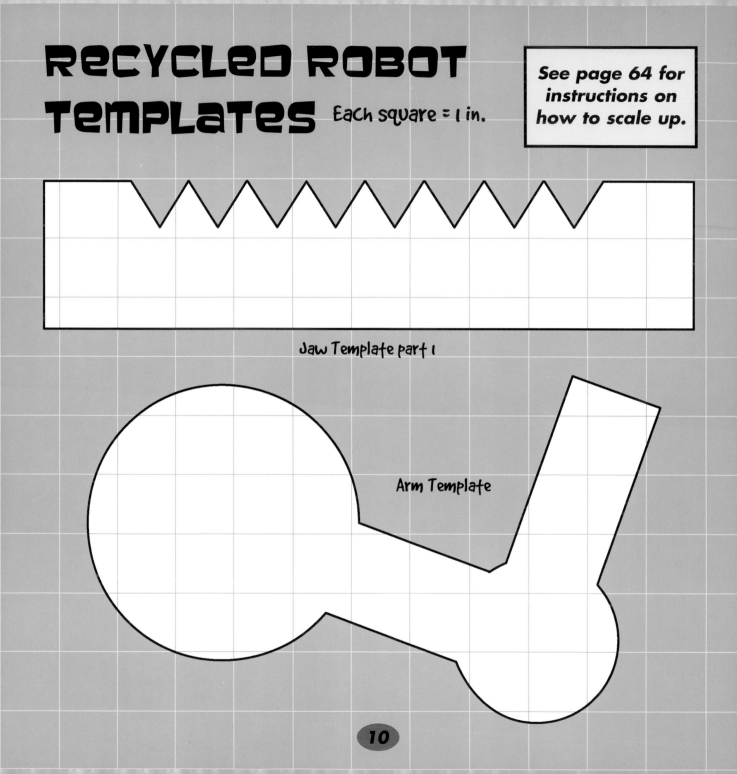

RECYCLED ROBOT
TEMPLATES

Each square = 1 in.

See page 64 for instructions on how to scale up.

Jaw Template part 1

Arm Template

10

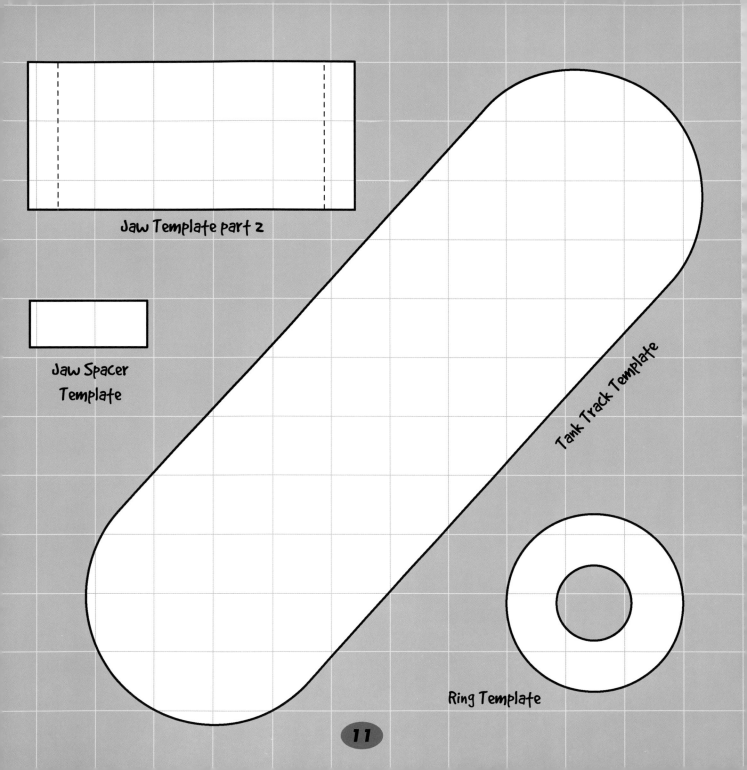

Jaw Template part 2

Jaw Spacer
Template

Tank Track Template

Ring Template

BOX FISH

With its snapping jaws and huge black mouth, this cardboard box fish makes a real splash. Its big eyes keep a lookout for any unsuspecting prey that swims too close, while those sharp-toothed jaws wait to gobble up your dirty laundry. Decorate the model in your favorite colors and its markings will send out a warning that this is one fish that won't end up battered with fries!

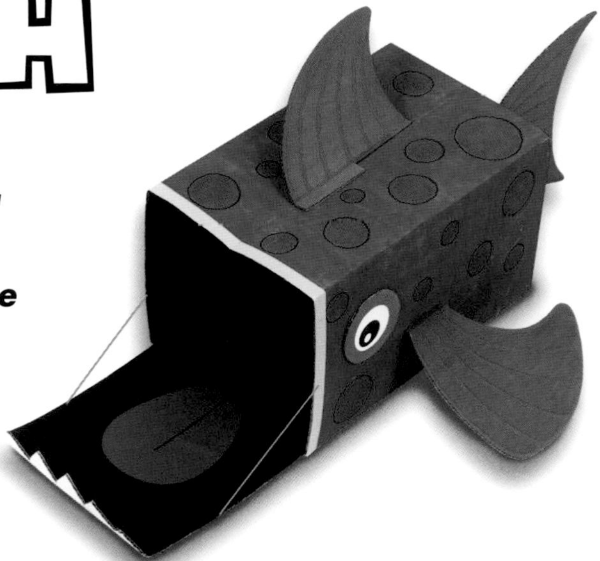

You Will Need:

One large rectangular box

Scissors

Tape

Thick card

White paper

Poster paint and paintbrushes

A pencil

A black marker pen

Red paper

Strong white glue

Two rubber bands

MAKING THE FISH

1 Find yourself a large rectangular cardboard box. Ask an adult to help you cut along the sides of one end to create a flap that is hinged at the bottom, as shown.

1

2 Use tape to secure the other box flaps shut firmly. Scale up and copy the tooth template (see page 16) onto card. Use this to draw a row of teeth onto the flap you created in step 1 and then cut out the teeth, as shown.

2

3 If the cardboard box you have found has print all over it, cover it up by gluing sheets of white paper over the outside of the box (including the teeth).

3

4

4 Paint the inside of the box black and paint the outside of the box orange. When the paint is dry, take a pencil and draw circles of different sizes all over the box to create a spotty pattern. Paint the circles purple. When they are dry, draw an outline around them all with a black marker pen.

5 Scale up and copy the two eye circle templates (see page 17). Draw the larger one onto a thick sheet of card twice, and the smaller one onto a piece of white paper twice. Ask an adult to help cut them out. Paint the two thick card circles a light purple. Draw eye details with a black marker pen onto the smaller paper circles. Glue the white paper circles onto the center of the larger thick card circles. Now glue the thick card circles onto either side of the box, as shown. Scale up and copy the tongue template (see page 16) onto a sheet of red paper. Cut this out, and add details to it with a black marker pen. Use glue to stick the tongue to the hinged flap you made in step 1.

6 Scale up and copy the side (two), top (one) and tail (one) fin templates (see pages 16–17) onto thick card. Cut them out with the help of an adult and paint them orange and purple, as shown. Use glue on the tabs of each fin to fix them in place on the cardboard box body, as shown.

7 Paint a light pink lip around the mouth of your fish, or use a thin strip of colored paper to achieve the same look, as shown. With a pencil, make four holes in your fish (two in the mouth flap and two in the box sides) and loop rubber bands through them, as shown, to create a snapping mouth.

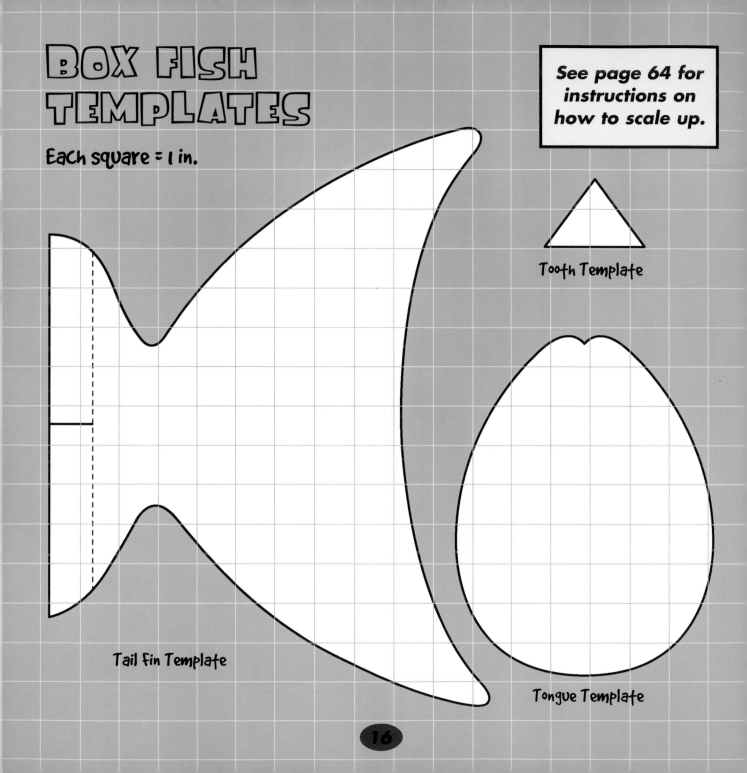

BOX FISH TEMPLATES

Each square = 1 in.

See page 64 for instructions on how to scale up.

Tooth Template

Tail Fin Template

Tongue Template

16

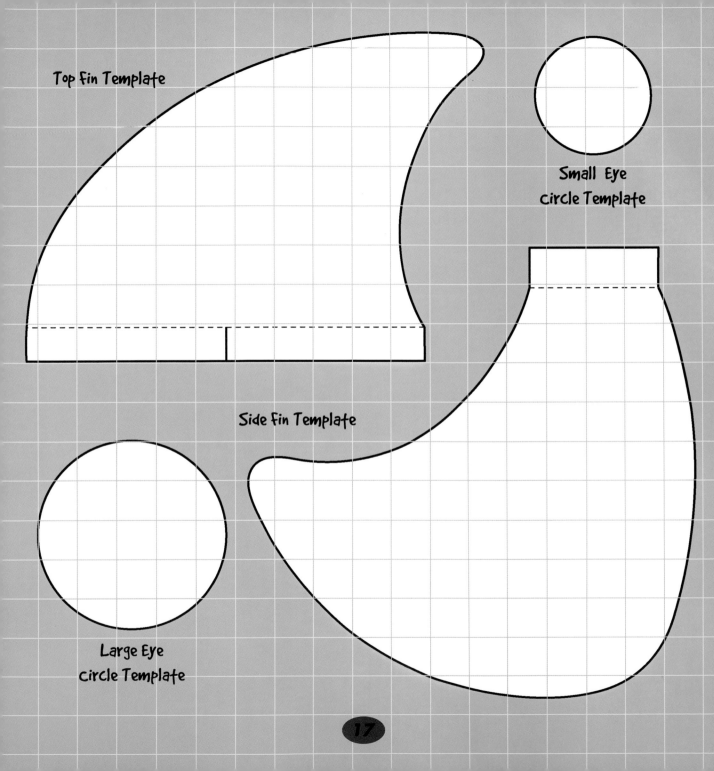

Top fin Template

Small Eye
circle Template

Side fin Template

Large Eye
circle Template

17

TOTEM POLE

With its colorful markings and feather headdress, it's hard to believe that this brilliant totem pole was once three chip cartons! Use it to store your favorite pens, pencils, erasers... whatever you like! The scary faces will ward off bad luck—and should keep prying friends and family away!

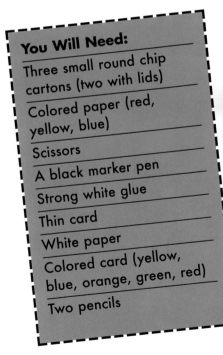

You Will Need:

Three small round chip cartons (two with lids)

Colored paper (red, yellow, blue)

Scissors

A black marker pen

Strong white glue

Thin card

White paper

Colored card (yellow, blue, orange, green, red)

Two pencils

MAKING THE TOTEM POLE

2 Cut six strips of colored paper that are 1 in. wide and long enough to go around the tubes. Make two red, two yellow, and two blue. Add details to the strips with a black marker pen. Glue the red strips to the yellow carton, the yellow strips to the blue carton, and the blue strips to the red carton.

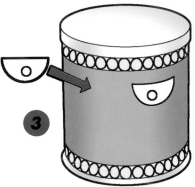

1 Find three small round chip cartons: two of them must have their lids. Cover up the printing by gluing a strip of colored paper around each one, as shown. (Make one red, one yellow and one blue.)

3 Scale up and copy the eye template (see page 23) onto thin card. Draw around it six times onto a sheet of white paper and cut them all out. Add details to each eye with a black marker pen. Glue two eyes onto each carton, as shown.

4 Scale up and copy the three nose templates. Draw around each one twice onto green card and then cut them out. Glue each pair together, leaving the tabs free of glue. Now glue the tabs of each nose onto a carton, as shown. Add different cheek and eyebrow details to each face with a black marker pen, as shown.

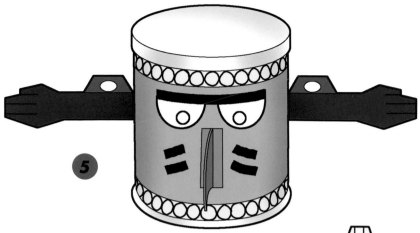

5 Scale up and copy the straight arm template (see page 23) onto red card and cut out two. Draw on fingers with a black marker pen and bend the tabs into shape. Use the tabs to glue an arm onto either side of the blue carton, as shown. Push its lid back on.

6 Scale up and copy the bent arm template (see page 23) onto yellow card and cut out two. Draw on fingers with a black marker pen and bend the tabs into shape. Use the tabs to glue an arm onto either side of the red carton, as shown. Push its lid back on.

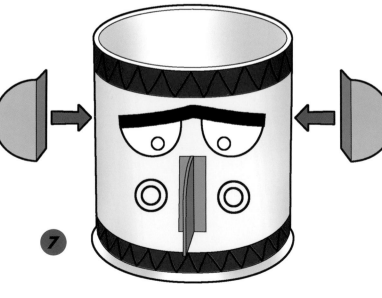

7 Scale up and copy the ear template (see page 23) onto blue card and cut out two. Draw on details with a black marker pen and bend the tabs into shape. Use the tabs to glue an ear onto either side of the yellow carton, as shown.

8 Scale up and copy the feather and circle templates (see page 23). Draw two feathers onto orange card and one onto red card and cut them out. Draw one circle onto green card and cut this out. Glue all these together, as shown, and add details with a black marker pen.

9 Glue the feather headdress made in step 8 onto the top of the yellow carton, as shown.

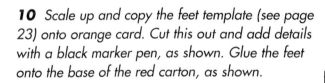

10 Scale up and copy the feet template (see page 23) onto orange card. Cut this out and add details with a black marker pen, as shown. Glue the feet onto the base of the red carton, as shown.

11 Place the cartons on top of one another, as shown. Ask an adult to help you cut out the holes marked in the arms and store your pencils here. You could keep your pens at the top and store your erasers, sharpeners and keepsakes in the bottom two heads.

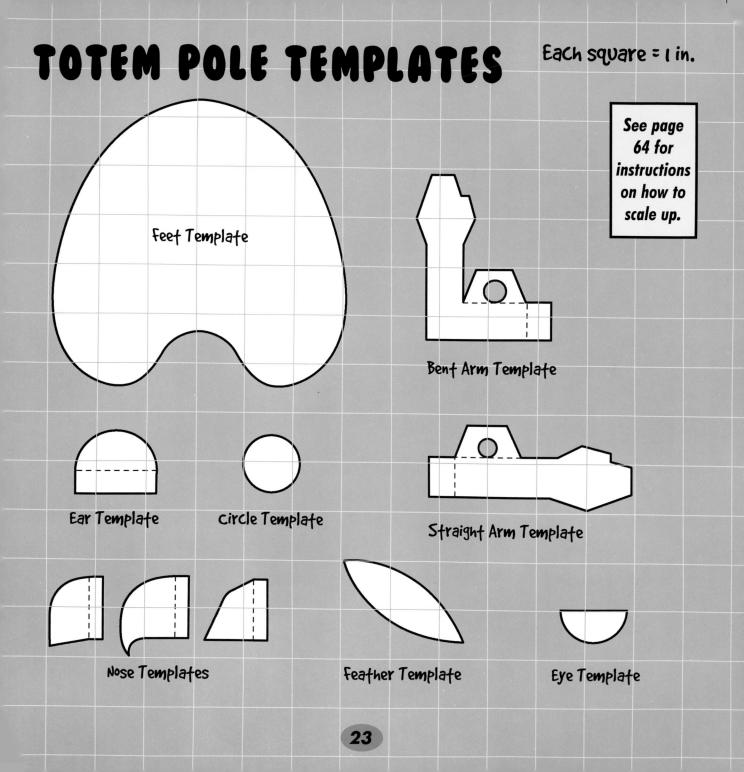

TOTEM POLE TEMPLATES

Each square = 1 in.

See page 64 for instructions on how to scale up.

Feet Template

Bent Arm Template

Ear Template

Circle Template

Straight Arm Template

Nose Templates

Feather Template

Eye Template

GLOVE PUPPETS

These three puppets are just a few of the creatures you can make using recycled gloves. An old pair can quickly be transformed into a couple of tortoises, or a single glove makes a snarling stegosaurus! Once you've made your puppets, you can entertain your family and friends by performing plays. Then, when you need some new characters, just have a look in a secondhand store for more materials.

STEGOSAURUS

You Will Need:

Thin green card

Scissors

Strong white glue

A black marker pen

An old woolly glove

Thin white card

Two small white buttons

TORTOISE

You Will Need:

Cereal box cardboard

Scissors

Strong white glue

Paint and paintbrushes

A pencil

A glove

Thin cardboard

A black marker pen

SPIDER

You Will Need:

Cereal box cardboard

A ball of black wool

A ball of orange wool

Scissors

A black woolly glove

A needle and black thread

Thin white card

A black marker pen

Strong white glue

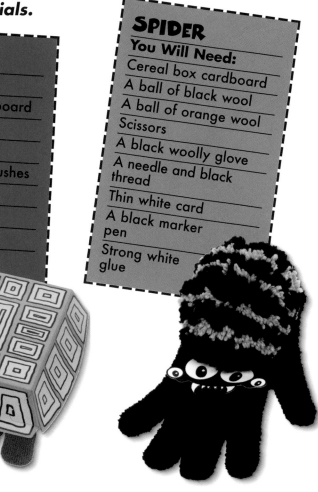

MAKING A STEGOSAURUS

1 Copy the five back plate templates (see page 30) provided onto a sheet of thin green card (you will need two sets). Carefully cut them out and bend the tabs into place.

2 Copy the tail template (see page 30) twice onto some thin green card. Cut these out and then glue them together, as shown.

3 Using a black marker pen, draw details onto each back plate and scales onto the tail, as shown.

4 Find an old woolly glove (ideally green, brown or gray in color). Using the tabs, glue the two sets of back plates onto the glove in this size order: small, medium, large, medium, small. Make sure the back plates line up along the middle of the glove.

5 Using the tabs, glue the tail onto the glove, as shown. Make sure that it lines up with the back plates. Copy the tail spike template onto some thin white card four times. Cut them out and glue them onto the end of the tail, as shown.

6 Using white glue, attach two small white buttons to the middle finger of the glove, to create eyes, as shown.

MAKING A TORTOISE

1 Copy the tortoise shell template (see page 31) onto a piece of cereal box cardboard. Carefully cut it out (including the circle at one end).

2 Ask an adult to help score along the dotted lines with a pair of scissors, bend the shell into shape and glue the tabs into place with glue.

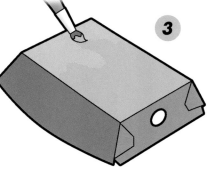

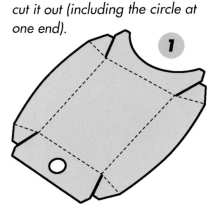

3 Paint the tortoise shell with a base coat of dark gray.

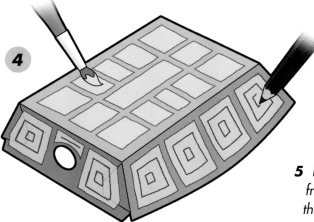

4 When the dark gray paint is dry, use a pencil to draw on a shell pattern. Paint this pattern a light gray color, as shown. When the light gray paint is dry, draw on the shell details, as shown.

5 Push the middle finger of an old glove through the hole in the front of the shell. Use the template to make a pair of eyes from thin cardboard. Add detail using a black marker pen. Glue the eyes on the glove's middle finger, to complete your tortoise.

MAKING A POM-POM SPIDER

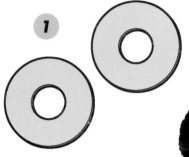

1 Copy the pom-pom template (see page 30) twice onto a piece of cereal box cardboard. Carefully cut out the circles.

2 Wind a ball of black wool until it will just squeeze through the hole in the middle of your pom-pom templates. Knot one end of the wool around your templates, as shown.

3 Carefully wind the wool around the templates, as shown. Keep going until you have completely covered the templates with black wool.

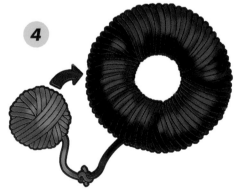

5 Repeat steps 3 and 4 so that you build up alternate layers of black wool and orange wool. Do this until the hole in the middle of the templates disappears. Now tie the end of the wool so that it will not come undone.

4 Now wind yourself a small ball of orange (or other brightly colored) wool. Knot this onto the end of the black wool and then repeat step 3 by winding the orange wool over the black wool until the black wool cannot be seen.

6 Take a pair of scissors and carefully snip through the layers of wool until you find the edges of the two cardboard templates. Pull these templates apart so that you can get your scissors in between them and then cut all the way around them, as shown. You may require adult supervision.

7 Take a length of black wool and slip it in between the two cardboard templates. Pull it tight and tie it in a knot so it holds all of the wool together. Now cut away the two cardboard templates. You should be left with a striped pom-pom.

8 Ask an adult to stitch your pom-pom onto the top of the black woolly glove, using a needle and black thread, as shown.

9 Copy the face template provided onto a sheet of thin white card and cut it out. Color it in and add some eyes to the circles, using a black marker pen. Glue this onto the glove with white glue, as shown, to complete your spider.

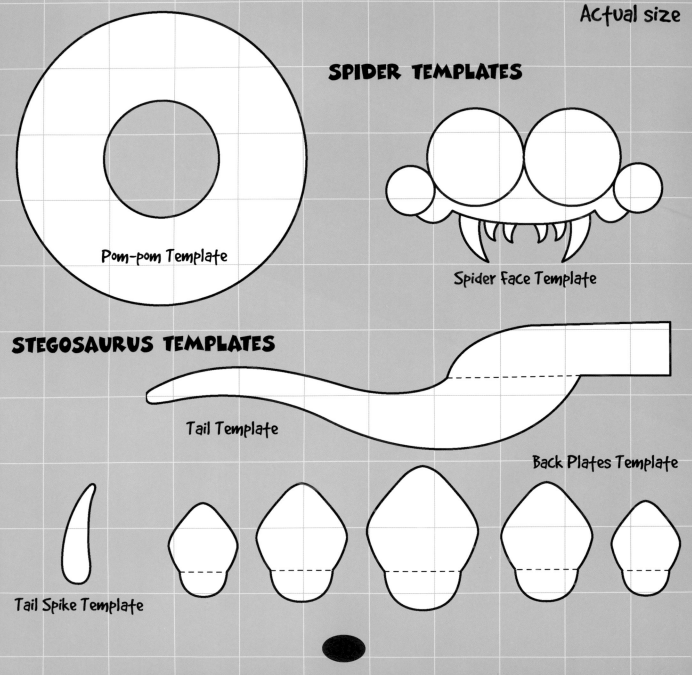

GLOVE PUPPET TEMPLATES

Actual size

SPIDER TEMPLATES

Pom-pom Template

Spider face Template

STEGOSAURUS TEMPLATES

Tail Template

Back Plates Template

Tail Spike Template

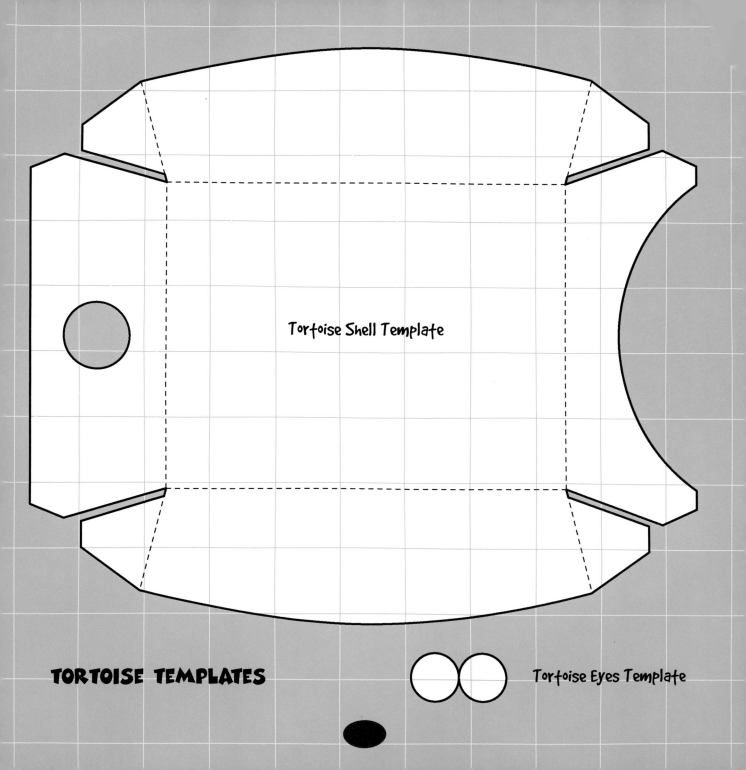

Tortoise Shell Template

TORTOISE TEMPLATES

Tortoise Eyes Template

KATY PILLAR

Three egg boxes form the different segments of this caterpillar's body and each of her eighteen feet wears little lace-up shoes! She's a cute creepy-crawly, and you can choose your favorite colors to decorate her body and bow. Dotty and spotty patterns look best, so get out your paintbrush and bring Katy the egg box caterpillar to life.

You Will Need:
Three egg boxes
Strong white glue
Scissors
Thin card
Paint and paintbrushes
A pencil
A black marker pen
Colored card (red, yellow and green)

MAKING KATY PILLAR

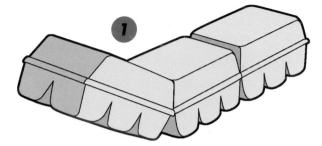

1 Take three egg boxes and glue all their lids shut. Tear off any labels that they have on them and glue all three of them together in a line with white glue, as shown.

2 Scale up and copy the back template (see page 35) onto a sheet of thin card. Glue this onto the egg boxes, as shown. (This will help to strengthen the egg boxes and hold them together, as well as covering any printing they may have on them).

3 Paint the egg boxes a bright pink color. When the pink paint is dry, take a pencil and draw circles of different sizes all over the caterpillar's back to create a spotty pattern. Paint the circles purple. When they are dry, draw an outline around each one with a black marker pen.

4 Scale up and copy the foot template (see page 35). Draw around this template ten times onto a piece of red card and eight times onto a piece of yellow card. Cut out all of the feet and add laces to them using a black marker pen.

34

5 Use white glue to stick the feet to the bottom of the egg boxes. Start at the front of the caterpillar with a pair of red feet, and then alternate between the two colors for each pair, as shown.

6 Scale up and copy the eyes, bow and tongue templates onto colored card. Draw on details with a black marker pen and then glue them in place on the front of your caterpillar, as shown.

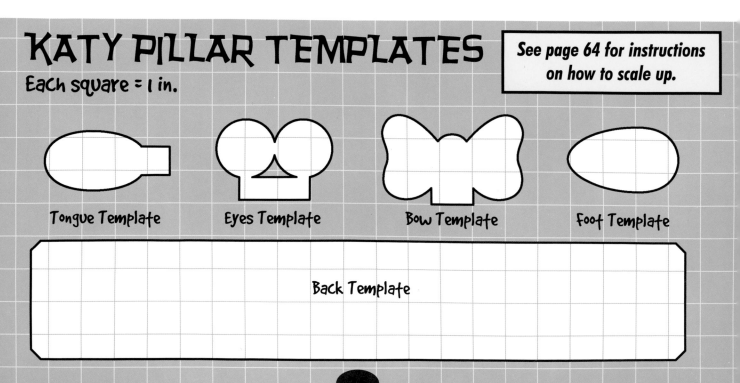

KATY PILLAR TEMPLATES

Each square = 1 in.

See page 64 for instructions on how to scale up.

Tongue Template

Eyes Template

Bow Template

Foot Template

Back Template

CEREAL BOX FLYERS

Cereal boxes provide some real airborne antics with these fantastic flyers. After finishing a delicious breakfast, instead of throwing away the box, transform it into a swooping, colorful bird or a soaring plane that would be the pride and joy of any air force. These flyers are quick and simple to make, and you can have some fun working up an appetite for your next bowl of cereal by taking them for a spin!

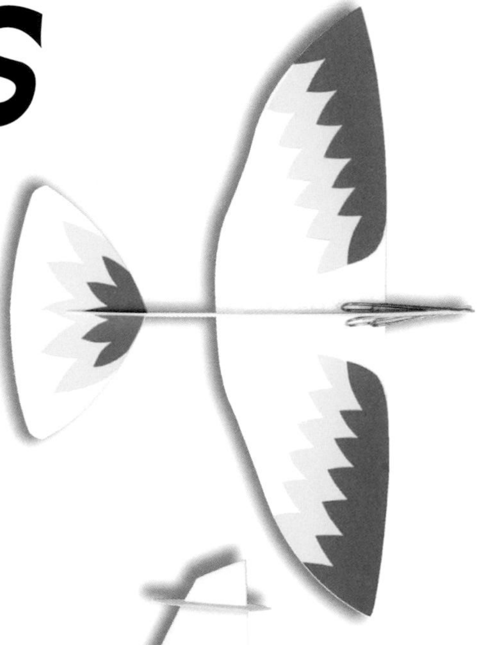

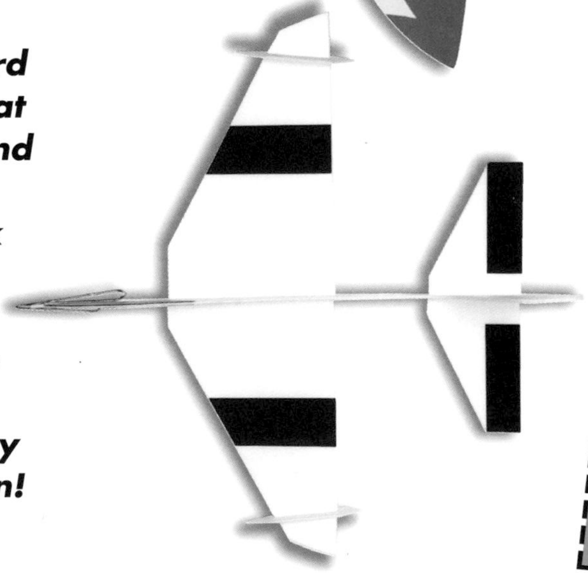

BIRD

You Will Need:

Thin card

A pencil

One cereal box

Scissors or craft knife

White paper (optional)

Thin colored paper

Strong white glue

One large paper clip

PLANE

You Will Need:

Thin card

A pencil

One cereal box

Scissors or craft knife

White paper (optional)

Strong white glue

One paper clip

Thin colored paper

MAKING A BIRD

1

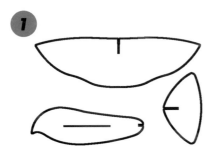

1 Copy the wing, tail, and body templates (see page 40) onto thin card and cut them out.

2

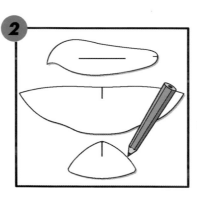

2 Using a pencil, carefully draw around the templates onto a cereal box. (You should be able to get all of the pieces out of one box).

3

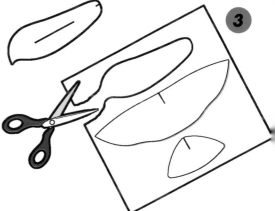

3 Carefully cut out all of these parts, including the slot lines. It is probably best to get an adult to do this for you. If they can cut them out with a craft knife, this will be even better. If your cereal box has print on it, cover it with white paper.

4

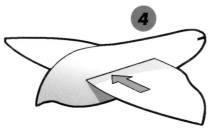

4 Push the wings through the large slot cut in the body of the bird.

5

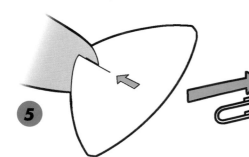

5 Push the tail onto the body by using the small slot cut at the rear of the body, as shown.

6

6 Decorate your bird with details made from thin colored paper, as shown. Glue them in place with white glue. Do not add too many as this may affect how well your bird will fly. Finally, add a large paper clip to the beak of your bird, as shown.

BUILDING A PLANE

1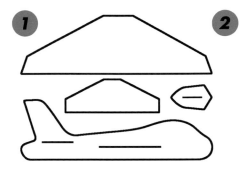

2

3

1 Scale up and copy the wing, tail, wing tips (two), and body templates (see page 41) onto thin card and cut them out.

2 Using a pencil, carefully draw around all of the templates onto a cereal box. (You should be able to get all of the pieces out of one box).

3 Carefully cut out all of these parts, including the slot lines. It is probably best to get an adult to do this for you. If they can cut them out with a craft knife, this will be even better. If your cereal box has lots of print on it, cover it with white paper.

4 Push the wings through the large slot cut in the body; and push the wing tips onto the ends of the wings, as shown.

6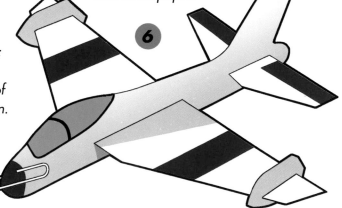

5 Push the tail through the small slot cut in the back of the body of the plane, as shown.

6 Decorate your plane with details made from thin colored paper, as shown. Glue them in place with white glue. Do not add too many as this may affect how well your plane will fly. Add a large paper clip to the front of your plane, as shown.

BIRD TEMPLATES Actual size

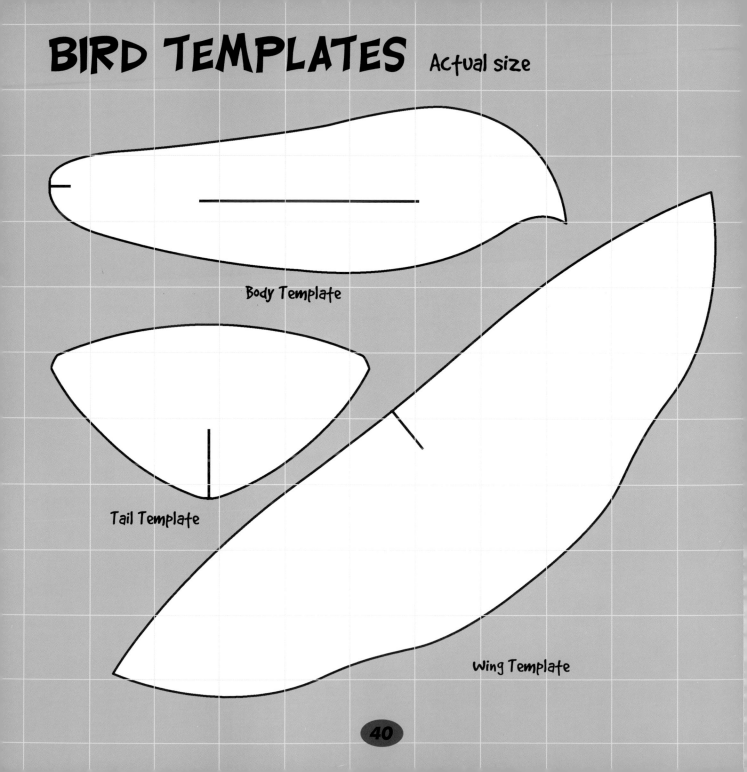

Body Template

Tail Template

Wing Template

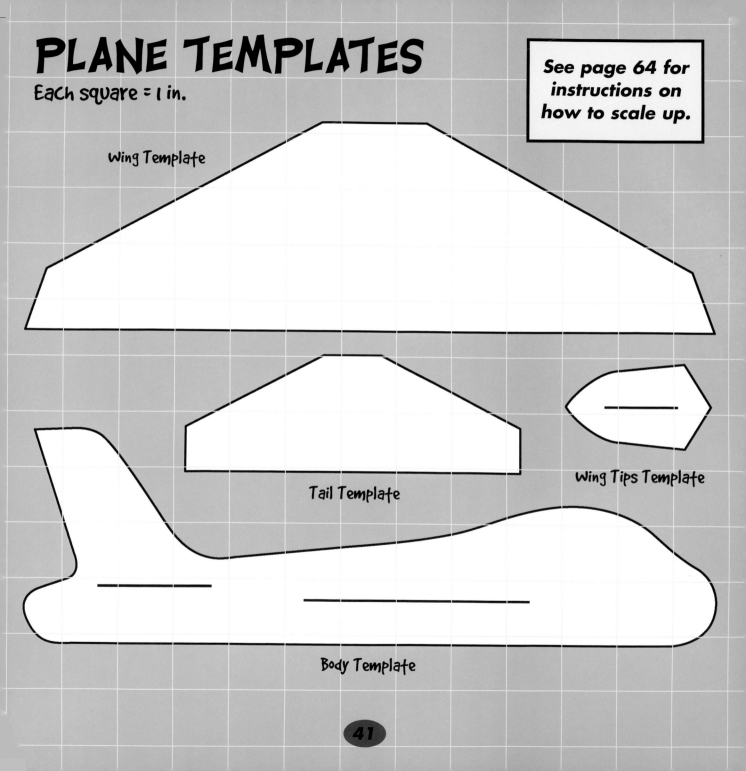

ROBOT SUIT

With this brilliant design for a robot suit made from trash, you can transform yourself into a real walking, talking robot! Follow the detailed instructions to construct the component parts, and watch as the whole thing comes to life. The more "bottle-top gadgets" you can add, the better it will be, so start looking in the kitchen for old bottle tops, containers, tubes and cartons!

You Will Need:

- Thick cardboard
- Scissors
- Masking tape
- Large and thin cardboard tubes
- Strong white glue
- Corrugated card
- Fabric softener bottle lid
- A square plastic container
- Two short yogurt cups
- Straws
- Paint and paintbrushes
- A black marker pen
- Colored candy wrappers
- One black, long-sleeved turtle-neck top or T-shirt
- Round plastic containers
- Plastic bottle tops
- Cereal box cardboard
- String
- Two large round chip containers
- Two plastic milk carton lids

ROBOT HEAD

1 Scale up and copy the head templates (see page 49) onto thick cardboard and ask an adult to help cut them out. Copy and cut out the two eye-hole markings on one of the head front/back templates.

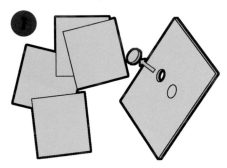

2 Scale up and copy the head support template onto a sheet of thick cardboard and ask an adult to help you cut it out. Wrap it around the top of your head, until it is a tight fit. Tape it together using masking tape, then stick it to the head top, as shown.

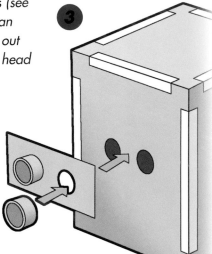

3 Using masking tape, fix the head front, back, sides and head top to one another to create the head shape, as shown. Make sure the head support, made in step 2, is fixed on the inside at the top. Scale up and copy the eye visor template onto thick card, and ask for adult help to cut it out. Cut two 1 in. segments from a large cardboard tube and glue them over the eye visor holes. Glue this to the head front, as shown.

4 Scale up and copy the jaw template onto thick card. Cut this out with adult help and score it where indicated, along the dotted lines. Using white glue, fix the jaw to the bottom of the head. Glue a strip of corrugated card 2 in. wide around the front and sides of the jaw, and glue a strip of corrugated card 1 in. wide around the entire top edge of the head. Cut two segments from a large cardboard tube that are 1/2 in. wide and glue these to either side of the jaw. Cut two circles of cardboard the same diameter as the tube. Glue one circle onto each tube segment, as shown.

5 Glue a fabric softener bottle lid onto the bottom of a square plastic container, then glue this on top of the head. Next, glue two short yogurt cups to either side of the head, then get adult help to cut out and glue two circles of thick card to the bottom of the yogurt cups. Finally, stick a straw onto each pot, as shown.

6 Paint the head red and light gray, as shown. Paint the fabric softener bottle lid yellow. When the paint is dry, add details to the jaw with a black marker pen. Complete the head by taping colored candy wrappers on the inside of the head over the eye holes.

ROBOT BODY

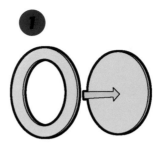

1 Scale up and copy the two body circle templates (see page 50) onto thick card and cut them out with adult help. Glue the ring-shaped one onto the solid one using white glue, as shown.

2 Glue the cardboard circles from step 1 onto the bottom of an old black long-sleeved top. Detail the center of the cardboard circles with a round container and plastic bottle top, as shown.

3 Paint three strips of corrugated cardboard, measuring 2 in. wide, light gray. When they are dry, glue them around the front and back of the top. Paint the cardboard circles, round container and plastic bottle top red, gray and blue, as shown.

ROBOT CHEST

1 Scale up and copy the chest pieces (see page 50) onto some thick cardboard and get adult help to cut out two of each. Using masking tape, fix the chest front, back, sides and tops to each other, as shown.

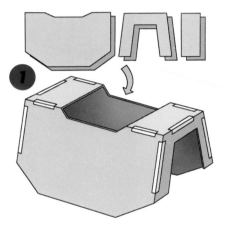

2 Scale up and copy the shoulder templates onto thick cardboard and get adult help to cut them out. Using masking tape, fix the shoulder top, middle, bottom and sides to one another to create the shoulders, as shown.

3 Attach the top of each shoulder to the sides of the chest by fixing strips of masking tape to either side of it, as shown. This should create a hinge that allows each shoulder to move. Then glue a strip of corrugated card, 2 in. wide, around the bottom edge of each shoulder, as shown.

4 Scale up and cut out the chest muscle panels and stick them in place on the front of the chest; on one of the panels glue another smaller rectangle-shaped panel. Cut two 3 in. long segments from a thin cardboard tube. Now cut each of the segments in half lengthways and glue them onto the tops of the chest, as shown. Next, find a small round plastic container and two plastic bottle tops. Glue the round container and bottle tops onto the chest muscles, as shown. Paint the completed chest red and light gray, as shown. Paint the round container purple and the two plastic tops yellow. When the paint is dry, add details with a black marker pen.

ROBOT KNEE/ELBOW JOINTS

1 Scale up and copy the knee/elbow joint (see page 51) onto a sheet of cereal box cardboard and cut out four. Bend each one into a cone shape and glue together using white glue and masking tape. Make a hole on either side of each cone (approx 1/2 in. from the base). Thread a piece of string approx 12 in. long through each of the holes and knot them on the inside, as shown. Finally paint the cones bright red and the strings black.

ROBOT ARMS

1 Take a large, round chip container and remove its lid. Using white glue, fix a 3 in. wide strip of corrugated cardboard around the bottom (solid end) of it, as shown. Next find two plastic milk carton lids. Glue these onto the chip carton, as shown. Ask for adult help to cut out a circle of thick card the same diameter as the solid end of the chip container and glue it on.

2 Scale up and copy the claw template (see page 51) onto some thick cardboard six times. Ask an adult to help you cut them out. Scale up and copy the claw support template onto a sheet of thin cardboard. Cut out and score it as indicated on the template and bend and glue it into shape, as shown. Glue all of the claws onto the claw support. Each claw shape must be glued onto one side of the claw support, as shown. Then stick the completed claw onto the solid end of the chip container, using tape or white glue.

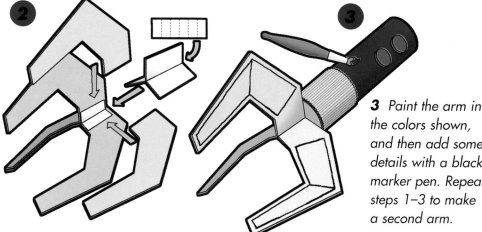

3 Paint the arm in the colors shown, and then add some details with a black marker pen. Repeat steps 1–3 to make a second arm.

ROBOT SHOES

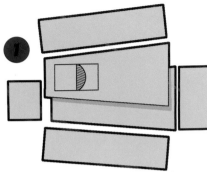

1 Scale up and copy shoe base (two), side (two), back (one) and front (one) templates onto thick cardboard. Carefully cut them out, with adult assistance.

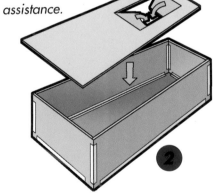

2 Copy the markings shown on the shoe base template onto one of the cardboard shoe bases. This will become the top of the shoe. Cut out and fold the markings to form an opening for your foot. Using masking tape, join all the pieces together to form a shoe shape.

3 Using white glue, fix a 2 in. wide strip of corrugated cardboard around the bottom of your basic shoe shape so it forms a sole.

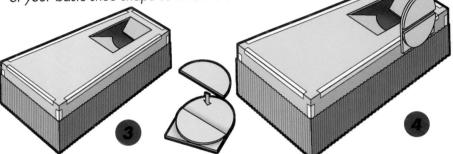

4 Scale up and copy the shoe bolt template (four) and the shoe bolt support template (two) onto a sheet of thick card. Cut them out, with some help from an adult. Using white glue, fix two shoe bolt parts onto each shoe bolt support. Glue the completed shoe supports onto either side of the shoe. Make sure that they line up with the opening in the top of the shoe, as shown.

5 Scale up and copy the shoe panel template onto a sheet of thick card and cut it out with some adult help. Glue it to the top of the shoe, as shown. Repeat steps 1–5 to make the second shoe. Paint your shoes in bright colors. When the paint is dry, add details with a black marker pen. Put lots of scrunched-up newspaper inside each shoe so that your feet fit snugly inside them.

ROBOT TEMPLATES

ROBOT HEAD TEMPLATES

Each square = 1 in.

See page 64 for instructions on how to scale up.

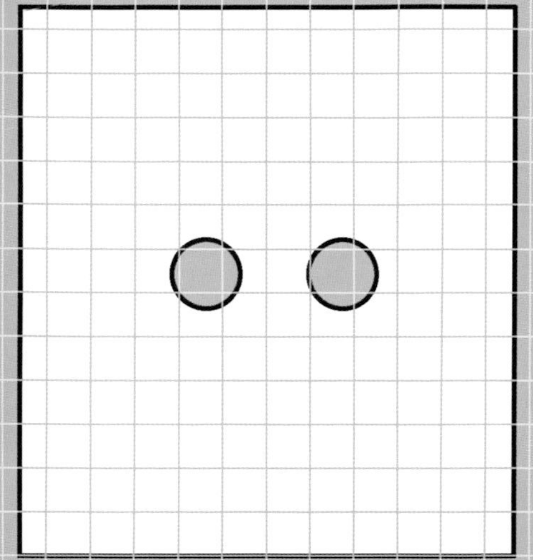

Head Front/Back

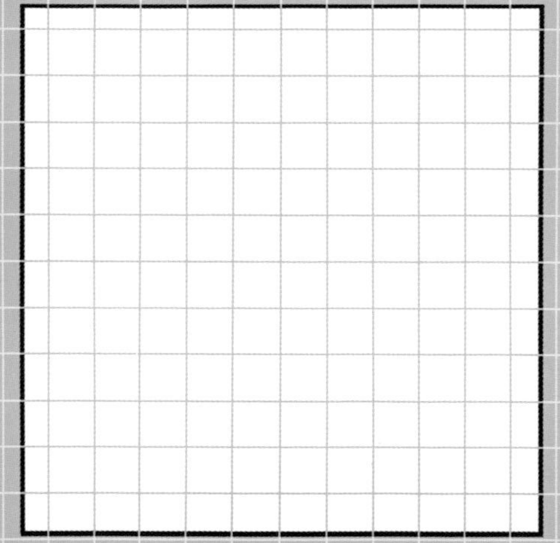

Head Top

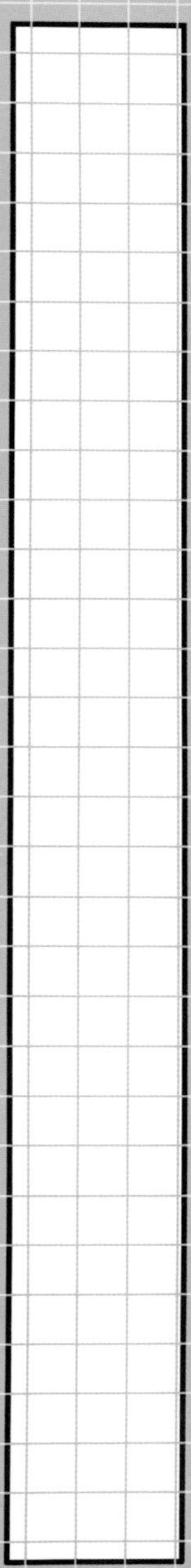

Head Support

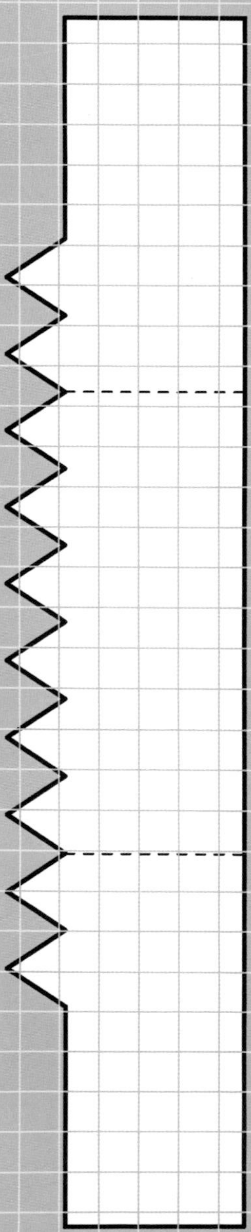

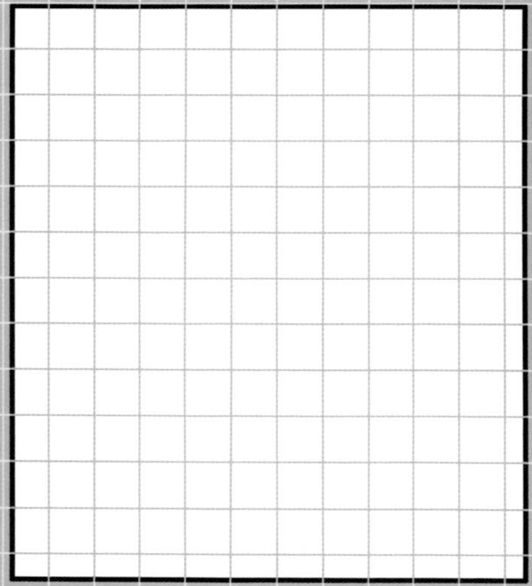

Head Side

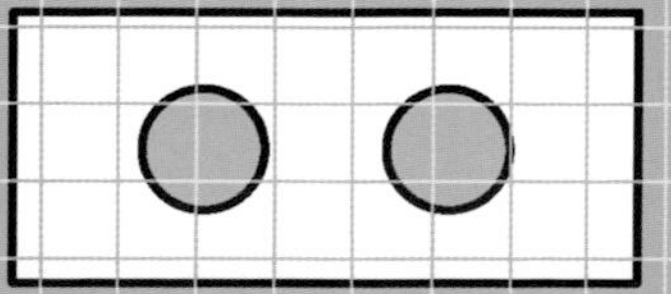

Eye Visor

Jaw

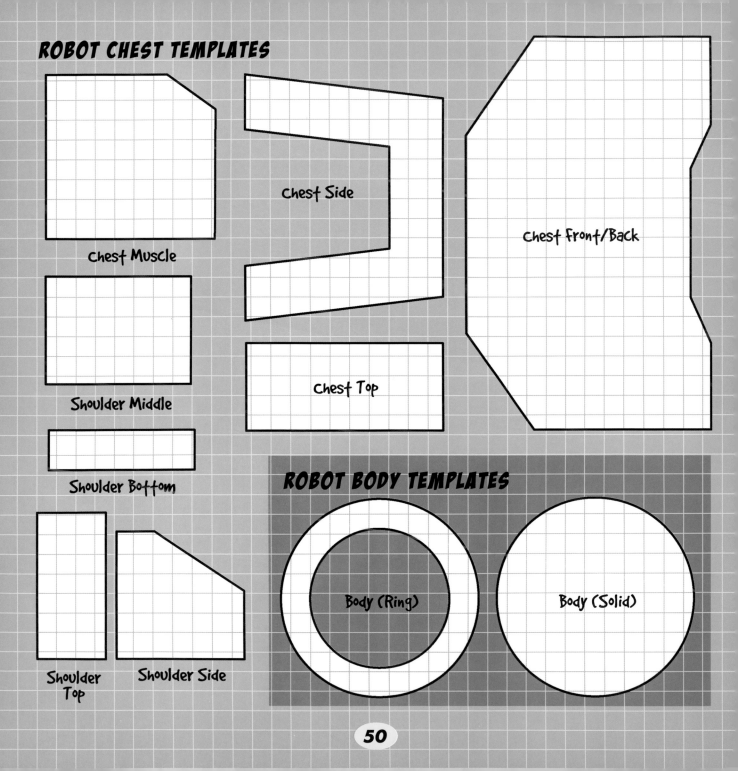

ROBOT CHEST TEMPLATES

Chest Muscle

Shoulder Middle

Shoulder Bottom

Chest Side

Chest Top

Chest Front/Back

Shoulder Top

Shoulder Side

ROBOT BODY TEMPLATES

Body (Ring)

Body (Solid)

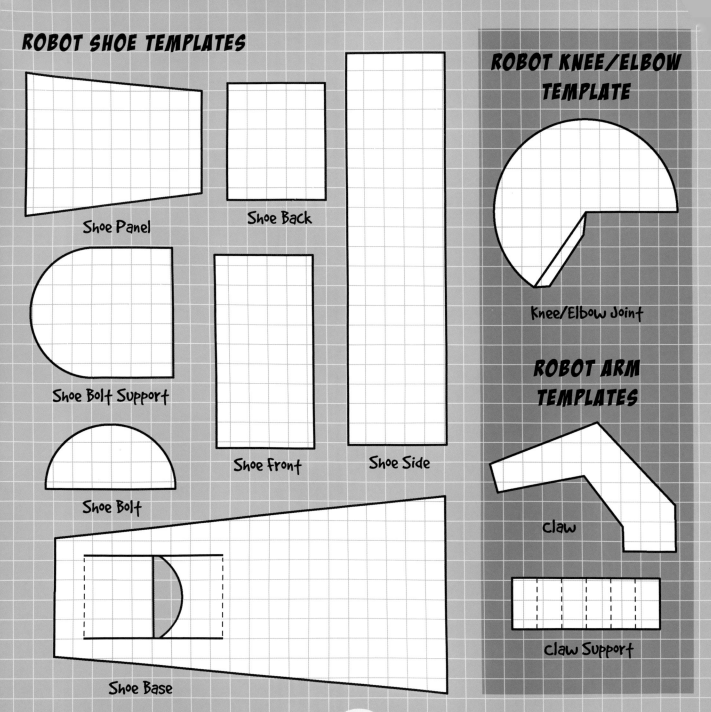

ROBOT SHOE TEMPLATES

Shoe Panel

Shoe Back

Shoe Bolt Support

Shoe Front

Shoe Side

Shoe Bolt

Shoe Base

ROBOT KNEE/ELBOW TEMPLATE

Knee/Elbow Joint

ROBOT ARM TEMPLATES

Claw

Claw Support

ALIEN SKITTLES

Make this fantastic game and you can bowl over hideous aliens with a fiery meteor from outer space! Challenge your friends to see who can get the highest score by knocking over these bug-eyed space invaders, then stand them back up and try again! It's as much fun making them as playing the game, so with each old bottle you manage to find, your alien army will continue to grow.

MAKING ALIEN SKITTLES

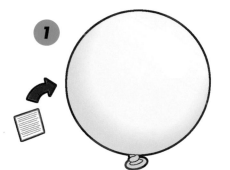

1 Inflate a balloon so that it is approx 4 in. across and round in shape. Tear a newspaper into small squares, roughly 1 in. x 1 in., and use wallpaper paste to cover the balloon with seven layers of papier mâché.

2 Tie a piece of string around the neck of the balloon, as shown, and hang it somewhere warm to dry.

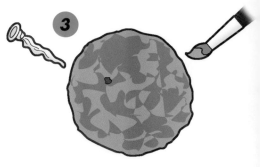

3 Once the papier mâché is dry, pop the balloon and remove it from the meteor shape. Paint the meteor with a base coat of dark purple. When it has dried, dry brush on a coat of light purple.

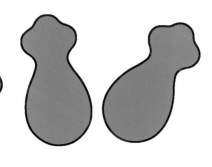

4 Find six clean, small soda bottles with lids. Pour a little paint (any color) into one of the bottles and tightly screw on the lid. Shake the bottle until the paint completely covers the inside of it. Then, in two of the bottles pour some more paint of a different color, and shake them. Repeat the action, using a different color, for the last three bottles.

5 Find three sheets of card that match the color of the paints you have used in the bottles. Scale up and copy the alien body template provided six times.

6 Scale up and copy the eye and stomach templates provided onto white paper. Draw twelve eyes and six stomachs. Cut them all out. Add details to the eyes and stomachs with a black marker pen. Glue a stomach to the front of every alien. Now glue three eyes onto four of the aliens. Draw shut eyes on two of the aliens and mouths on all of them with a black marker pen. Use white glue to fix each cardboard alien onto the correct color bottle. (You could paint numbers on each alien if you wish, as this will make scoring more exciting!)

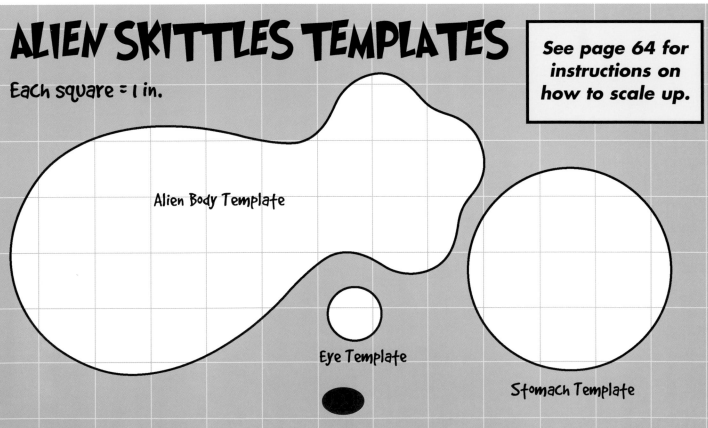

ALIEN SKITTLES TEMPLATES

See page 64 for instructions on how to scale up.

Each square = 1 in.

Alien Body Template

Eye Template

Stomach Template

TRANSPORTER PLANE

The main construction materials for this impressively large plane are two empty plastic water bottles and some cardboard. It's a fantastic model and includes some clever details, such as the engines made from small bottles and propellers created from plastic lids. Take your time painting the authentic colors and adding more details to the bodywork with a black marker pen, and you'll be rewarded with a plane that looks just like the real thing!

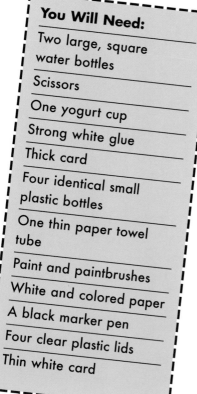

You Will Need:

Two large, square water bottles

Scissors

One yogurt cup

Strong white glue

Thick card

Four identical small plastic bottles

One thin paper towel tube

Paint and paintbrushes

White and colored paper

A black marker pen

Four clear plastic lids

Thin white card

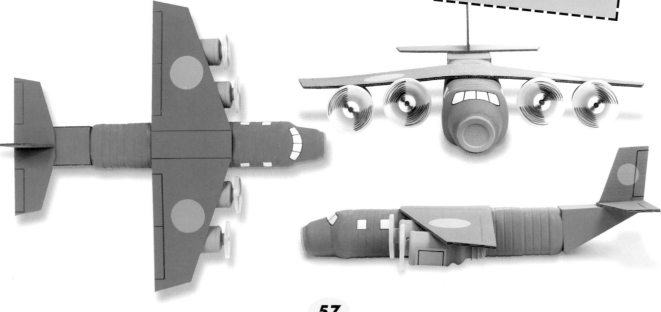

BUILDING A TRANSPORTER PLANE

1 Find two large water bottles that are square in shape. Cut the top off one of them and the bottom off the other one, as shown.

2 Using scissors, make a cut approx 1 in. long at each corner of the bottle with the bottom removed. Now carefully cut the neck off the bottle, as shown. Push this bottle onto the other one until you get a firm fit.

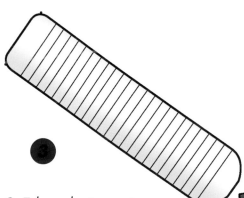

3 Take a short yogurt cup and ask an adult to neatly cut 1/2 in. off the top so that you get rid of its lip. Use white glue to glue the yogurt cup to the bottles from step 2, as shown.

4 Copy the wing template (see pages 62–63) onto a sheet of thick card twice and cut them out. Glue the two wing shapes together, then glue this onto the middle of the bottles with white glue. Leave to dry.

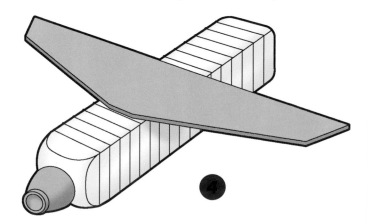

5 Copy the two tail templates onto thick card. (You will need two small tail templates and one large tail template. Ask an adult to help you.) Cut them all out and then glue them together, as shown.

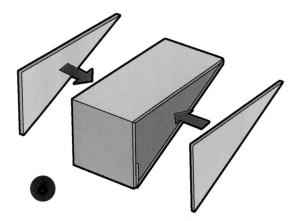

6 Copy the two rear body templates onto thick card. (You will need two small rear body templates, and one large rear body template.) Cut them all out and then glue them together, as shown.

7 Glue the tail you made in step 5 onto the rear body you made in step 6. When this is dry, glue the rear body onto the bottom of the bottles, as shown.

8 Find four identical small plastic bottles. Lay your plane upside down so that you can see the underneath of the wings. Glue two bottles onto each wing with white glue. It is important you make sure that each bottle sticks out over the front of the wings, and that they are evenly spaced, as shown.

9 Take a thin cardboard paper towel tube and carefully cut four sections from it that are each 1 in. long. Glue one of these sections onto each of the bottles that are attached to the wings, as shown.

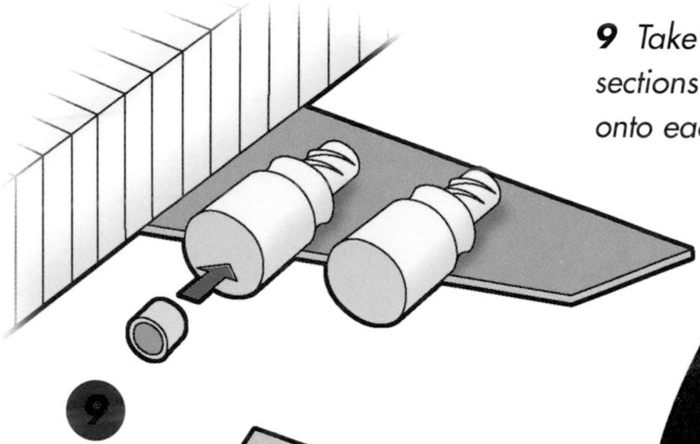

9

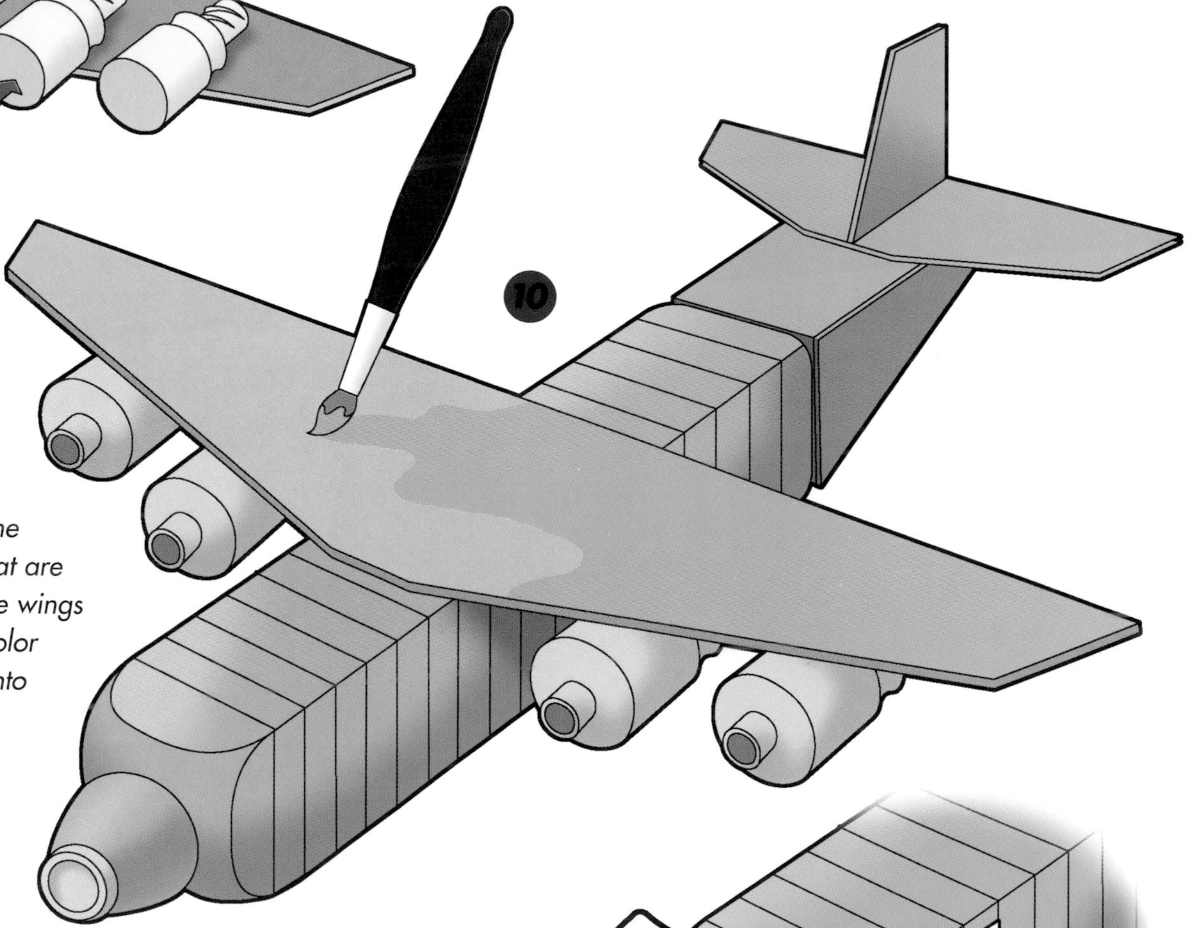

10

10 Paint your plane green. Paint the four bottles that are attached to the wings a light gray color to turn them into engines. Also paint the nose of the plane a light gray.

11 Using sheets of white and colored paper, design and glue onto the plane some windows, wing/tail markings, and engine panels, as desired.

11

12 Take a black marker pen and add panel lines, door hatches, and wing/tail flaps to your plane.

13 Find four clear plastic lids, such as those found on round chip cartons. With a black marker pen, draw the pattern shown on each to create the effect of spinning propellers.

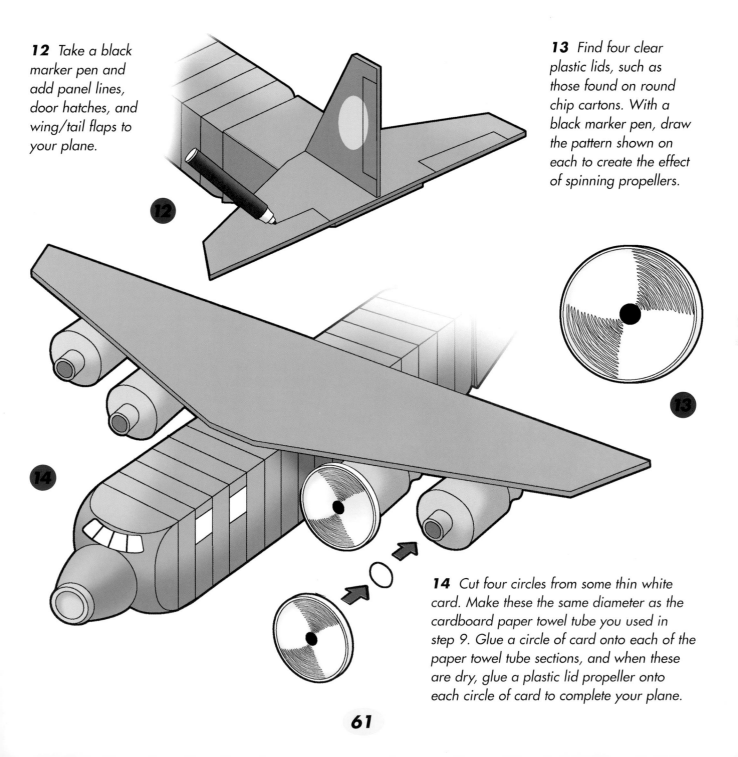

14 Cut four circles from some thin white card. Make these the same diameter as the cardboard paper towel tube you used in step 9. Glue a circle of card onto each of the paper towel tube sections, and when these are dry, glue a plastic lid propeller onto each circle of card to complete your plane.

TRANSPORTER PLANE TEMPLATES

Actual size

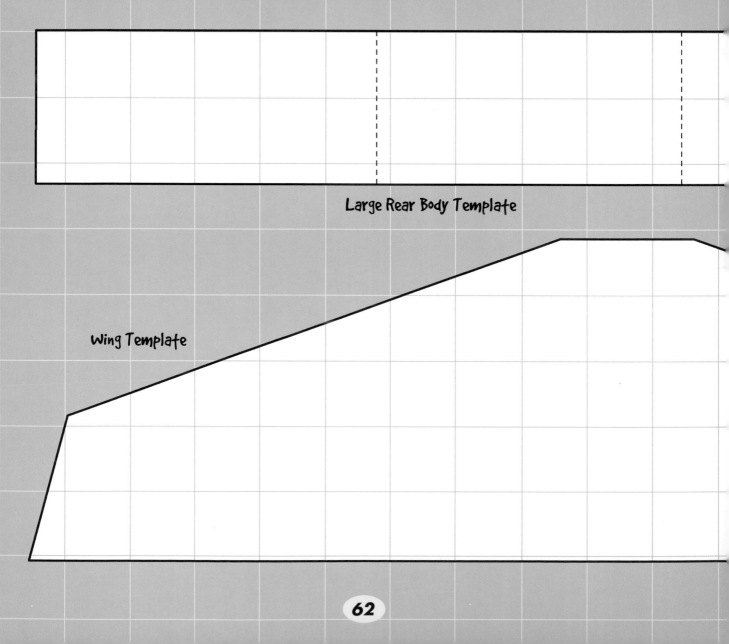

Large Rear Body Template

Wing Template

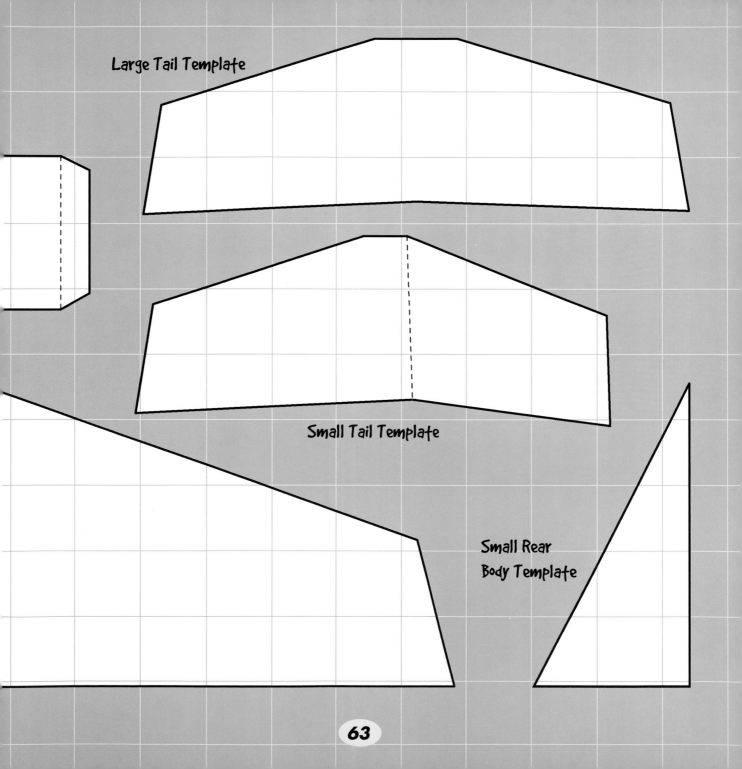

Large Tail Template

Small Tail Template

Small Rear
Body Template

GLOSSARY OF TERMS

SCALING UP

Throughout this book the term **scale up** is referred to when you need to draw up the templates. This just means drawn up bigger than they appear on the page.

All the squares on the template pages are equal to a 1 in. measurement, although on the pages they appear smaller. So you need to draw up a grid of squares that measure 1 in. on all sides, onto a piece of paper. Then, using a pencil and ruler, carefully copy what you see on the template page into each square of your grid.

Some projects are already the right size and won't need scaling up. For these you can use tracing paper to copy them straight from the page.

Cereal Box Cardboard—A sheet of cardboard made by flattening an old cereal box.

Cone—A shape formed by a circular base with even sides that meet at a top point above the base.

Corrugated—A surface that has alternating folds and ridges.

Craft knife—A very sharp knife that's used for cutting craft materials.

Diameter—The measurement across a circle.

Dry brush—Loading a paintbrush with a very small amount of paint, wiping it on a cloth, then painting onto a model to bring out the detail.

Hinge—A pivotal point that allows a part to move.

Joint—The point at which two pieces are joined together.

Marker pen—A pen that is used for adding finishing details to a model.

Masking tape—Tape that's usually used to cover areas not to be painted.

Papier-mâché—Hundreds of small pieces of paper stuck onto a surface with wallpaper paste to form a tough shell when dry.

Score—Using the blunt edge of a scissor blade to press down and make a line or crease in cardboard, allowing it to fold more easily.

Segment—The separate parts into which something can be divided.

Tab—A small flap on a part of a model that is covered with glue before being stuck to the model.

Templates—Guide pieces or patterns that are placed onto a material, usually cardboard, then drawn around to give the final shape.

White glue—A strong glue that is used for both DIY and crafts.